Goods or Services?

Ellen K. Mitten

ROURKE PUBLISHING
www.rourkepublishing.com

www.rourkepublishing.com

PHOTO CREDITS: Cover: © Rosemarie Gearhart; Title Page: © Gene Chutka; Page 3: © William Wang, Page 5, 22: © Catalin Peloea; Page 7: © PIKSEL; Page 9,17, 22: © kristian sekulic; Page 11: © Gennadiy Poznyakov; Page 13, 22: © Dean Mitchell; Page 15: © Catherine Yeulet; Page 19: © Christine Glade; Page 21: © kzenon; Page 22: © Rmarmion, © WendellandCarolyn, © Dimos

Edited by: Meg Greve

Cover design by Tara Ramo
Interior design by Renee Brady

Library of Congress Cataloging-in-Publication Data

Mitten, Ellen K.
 Goods or Services / Ellen K. Mitten.
     p. cm. -- (Little World Social Studies)
 Includes bibliographical references and index.
 ISBN 978-1-61741-791-7 (hard cover) (alk. paper)
 ISBN 978-1-61741-993-5 (soft cover)
 Library of Congress Control Number: 2011924836

Rourke Publishing
Printed in the United States of America, North Mankato, Minnesota
060711
060711CL

www.rourkepublishing.com - rourke@rourkepublishing.com
Post Office Box 643328 Vero Beach, Florida 32964

Have you ever wondered how families use **money**?

Families use money to buy **goods** and **services**.

Goods are things that we buy such as food, clothes, cars, and toys.

Services are things we pay someone else to do. When you visit the dentist, you are buying a service.

Other services you buy are activities such as movies, haircuts, and swimming lessons.

Most families must make **choices** on what goods and services to buy.

13

Families need to buy places to live, food to eat, ways to get to work and school, and clothes to wear.

Families want to buy things such as vacations, televisions, and tickets to the movies.

Every day, families **contribute** to the economy through their **spending** on goods and services.

Can you think of some of the goods and services your family buys?

Picture Glossary

 **choices** (CHOY-sizs): Items or activities that a person must decide between for purchase or use.

 **contribute** (kuhn-TRIB-yoot): To give money or provide help to make something better.

 **goods** (gudz): Things that are sold, or things that someone owns, as in leather goods or household goods.

money (MUHN-ee): The coins and bills that people use to buy things.

services (SUR-viss-iz): Jobs or work that helps others, such as cleaning houses, washing cars, or babysitting.

spending (SPEND-ing): Using money to make purchases.

Index

Websites

www.moneyoplis.org
www.orangekids.com
www.federalreserveeducation.org

About the Author

Ellen K. Mitten has been teaching four and five year-olds since 1995. She and her family love reading all sorts of books!